MyRobots Sticker

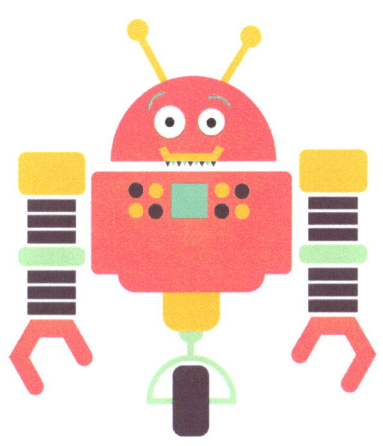

MyRobots Sticker

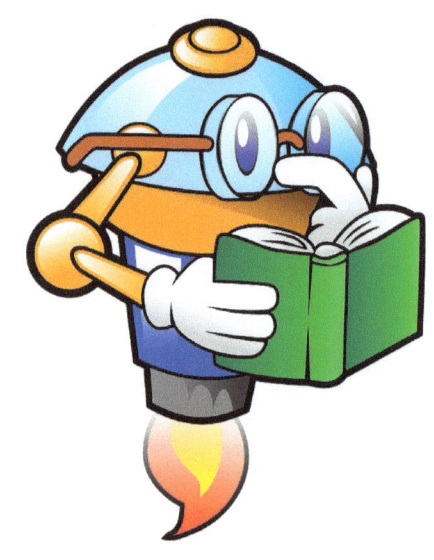

MyRobots Sticker

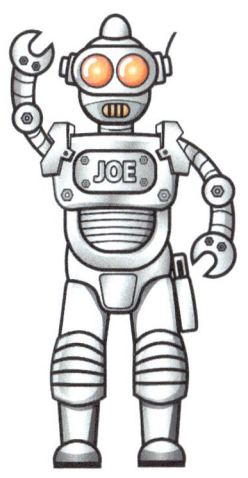

MyRobots Sticker

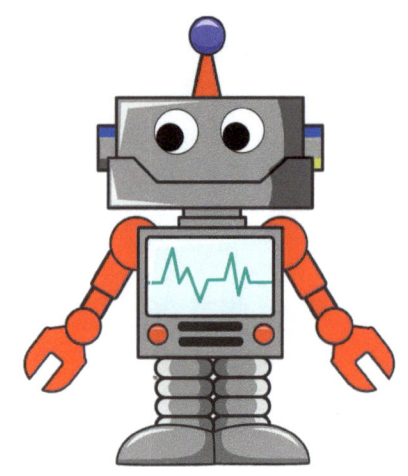

MyRobots Sticker

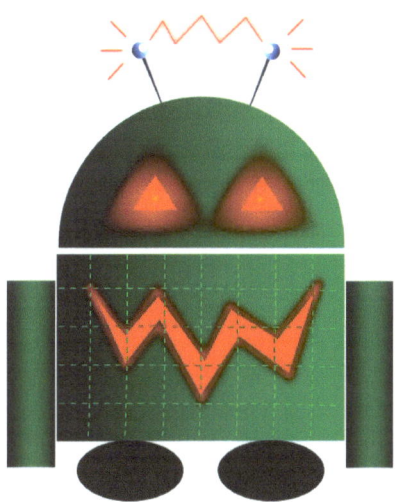

MyRobots Sticker

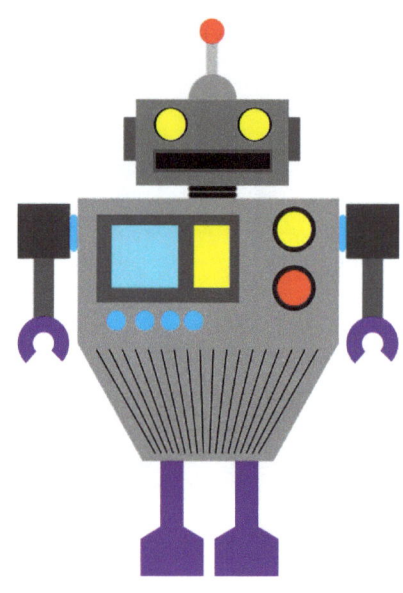

MyRobots Sticker

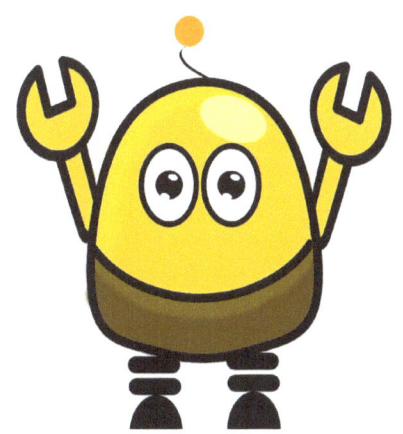

MyRobots Sticker

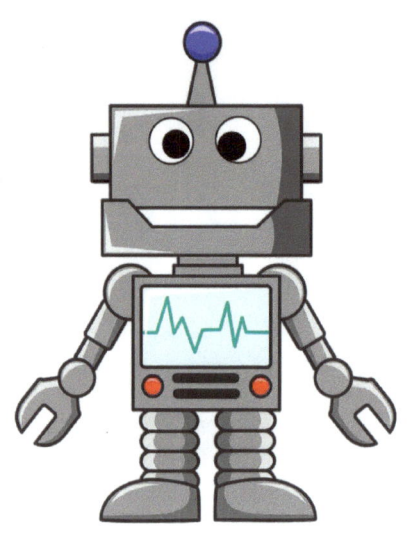

MyRobots Sticker

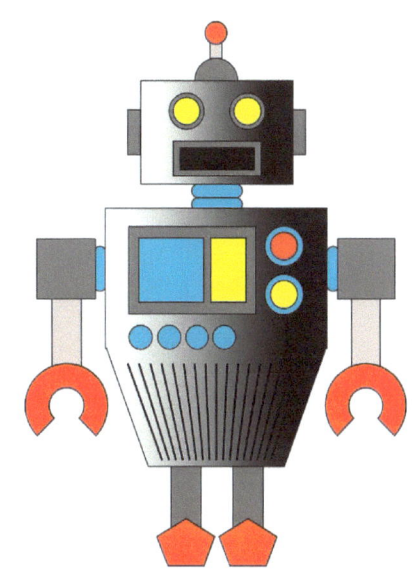

MyRobots Sticker

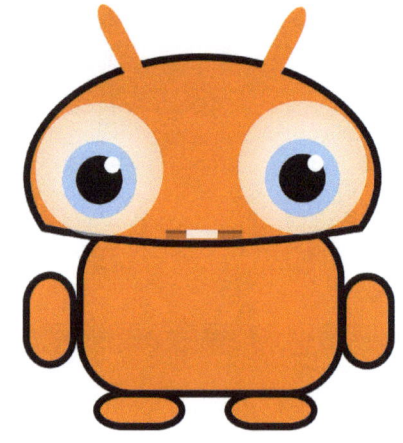

MyRobots Sticker

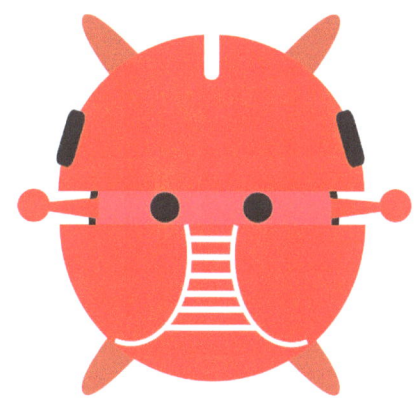

MyRobots Sticker

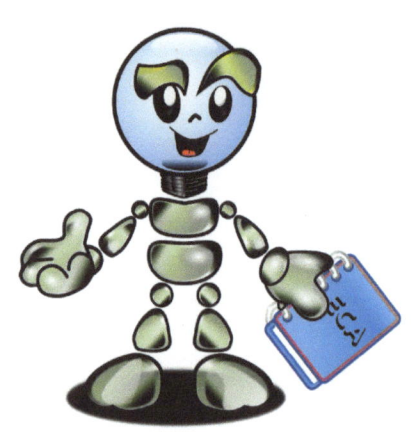

MyRobots Sticker

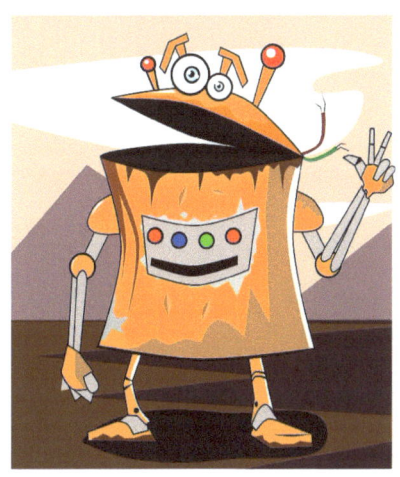

MyRobots Sticker

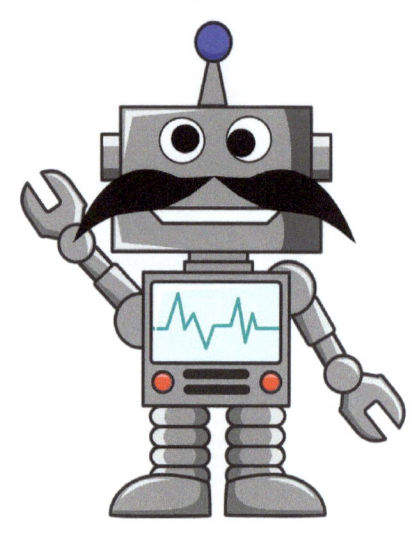

MyRobots Sticker

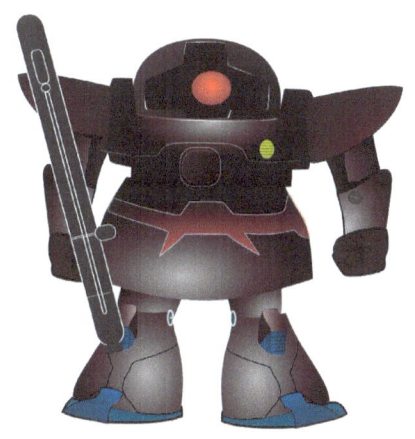

MyRobots Sticker

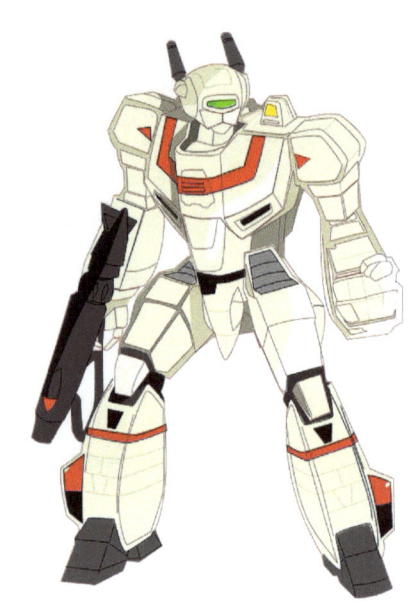

MyRobots Sticker

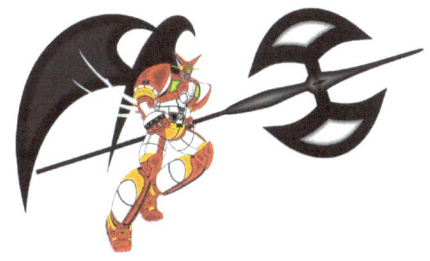

MyRobots Sticker

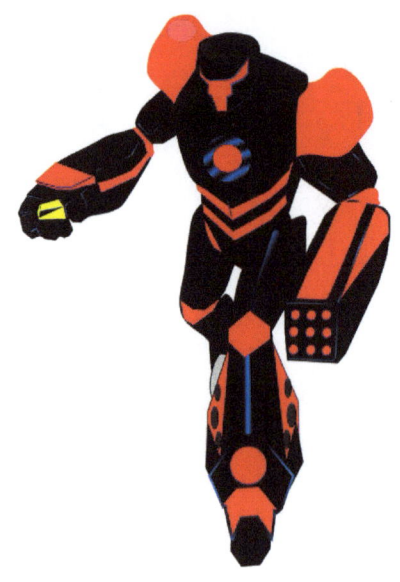

MyRobots Sticker

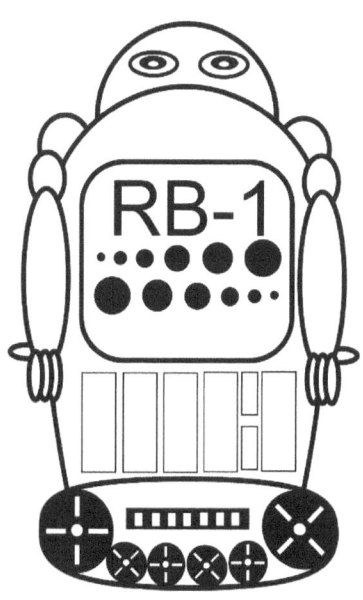

MyRobots Sticker

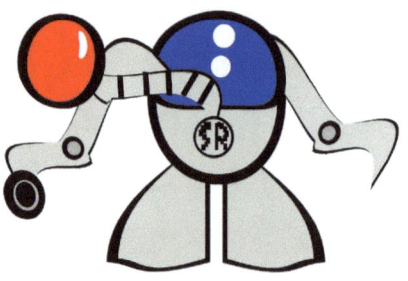

MyRobots Sticker

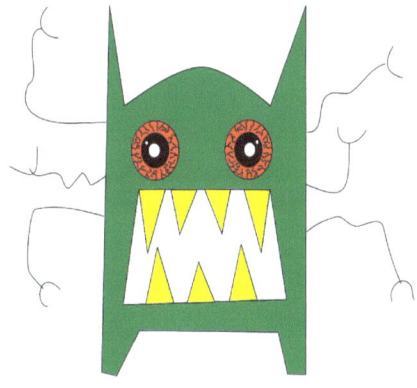

MyRobots Sticker

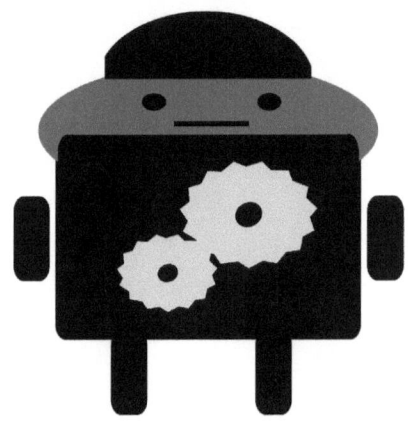

MyRobots Sticker

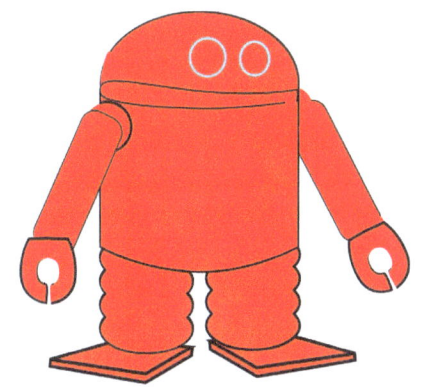

MyRobots Sticker

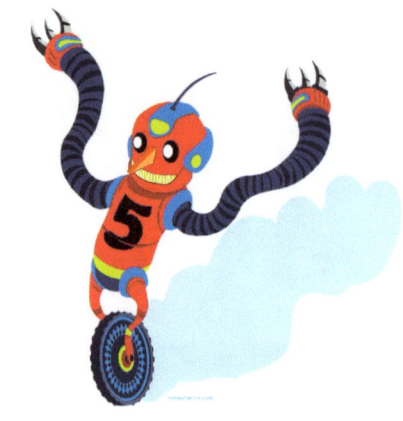

MyRobots Sticker

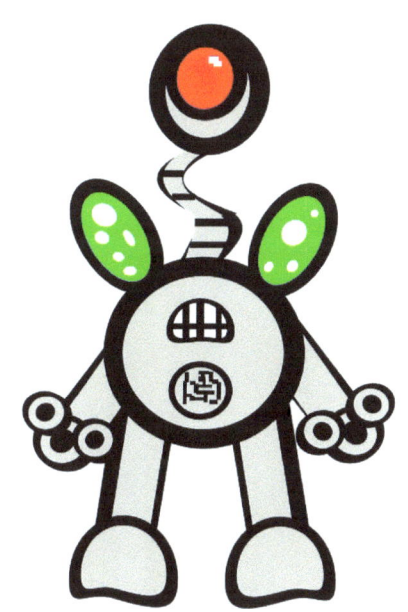

MyRobots Sticker

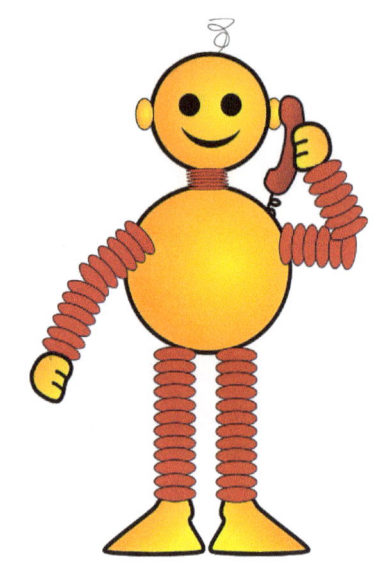

MyRobots Sticker

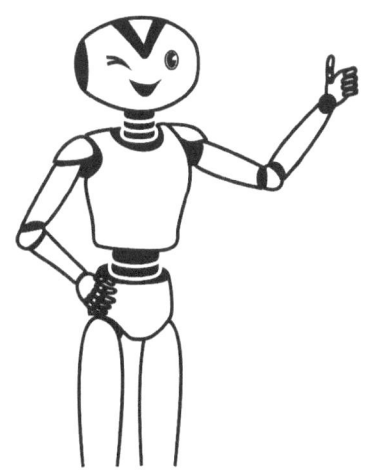

MyRobots Sticker

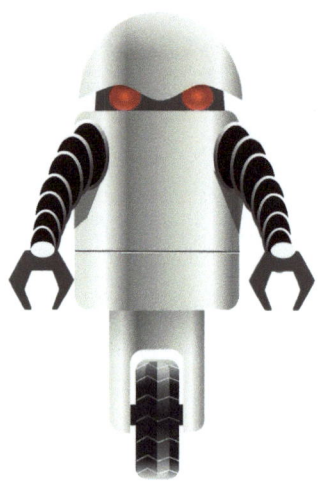

MyRobots Sticker

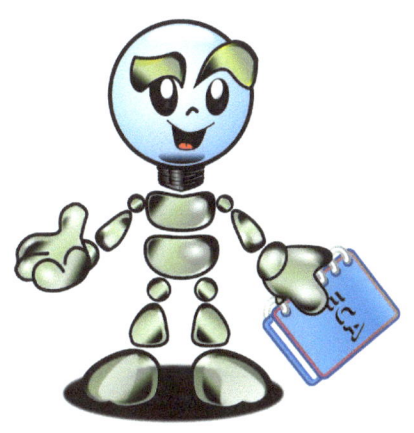

MyRobots Sticker

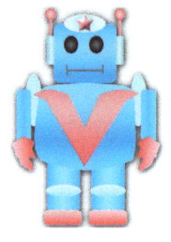

www.ingramcontent.com/pod-product-compliance
Lightning Source LLC
Chambersburg PA
CBHW051826210526
45473CB00005B/1751